# These REMEMBER

## · COLONIAL LIFE IN AMERICA ·

BY CAREN B. STELSON

ILLUSTRATED BY DAVID G. KLEIN

MODERN CURRICULUM PRESS

Pearson Learning Group

T hese shoes are old and cracked. They were made the old way, with the right shoe exactly the same as the left. They may look useless to you, sitting there in the town museum. But after 250 years, they still serve a purpose. Their job is to make you curious.

Do you wonder whose feet walked in these shoes? Do you wonder where they went every day? Maybe you wonder what it would be like living back when these shoes were new.

If so, you can follow these shoes back into history. Follow them to Colonial America when the land was rugged and wild. Head north to New England. Don't stop until you hear the clopping of horseshoes and the creaking of wagon wheels.

Once in town, you'll pass the meeting house. You'll pass the blacksmith shop. On the left are the general store and the town green.

Those wooden beams on the green are the stocks. People who break local laws have to stand with their heads and wrists locked in the stocks. One law says you can't gossip. Another says you can't use bad words. Luckily, there is no one in the stocks today.

Keep going. When you reach the printing shop, take the narrow dirt road out of town. Every man who lives here is supposed to work on the roads a few days a month. Most roads are still rutted and rough.

Keep the river on your right. You'll catch a glimpse of the grist mill, where grain is ground into flour. Then you'll see the Shaw farm.

Follow the path up to the Shaw house. This is where you'll find those shoes you saw in the museum. But something has changed. The shoes are brand new, and now they have feet in them.

The boy wearing those shoes has just finished feeding the chickens. His little sister runs about looking for hens' eggs in the dried grass. She finds one and places it carefully in her basket.

Just then a mother in a white cap sticks her head out the door. "Ezra! Charity! Come inside now."

Go ahead. Go inside with Ezra and Charity. Don't worry. No one will see you. You're invisible.

It's September. Outside, the warm summer breeze has turned crisp. Inside, it is cozy. Head over to the fireplace. Warm your hands and take a seat on the "settle." As you sit down, you may notice that the seat is very hard. The back is high and uncomfortably hard too. Ezra and Charity sit quietly next to you. They don't complain. They know this is the warmest spot in the house.

N ow that your hands are warm, stand up and have a look around, if you like. To your surprise, the whole house is one big room. The large stone fireplace takes up most of the wall in front of you. Hanging over the fire is a large iron kettle bubbling with rabbit stew. Dried herbs, apples, and pumpkins hang from pegs nearby.

You turn slowly to take in the rest of the room. A homemade bed fills one corner. Underneath it hides a small trundle bed, waiting for a sleepy child.

A ladder leads to a loft where Ezra and Charity sleep. You take a step back to have a better look. Oops! Don't stumble into that grandmother rocking a whimpering baby to sleep.

You turn again. Next to you is Charity. She's setting a long pine table with pewter mugs, wooden trenchers, and wooden spoons.

The latch clicks and the rugged wooden door opens. In stomp four older sons and a father. They hang their coats and three-cornered hats on wall pegs. The smell of stew meat fills the air as the whole family begins their midday meal.

All their clothes are very plain. No one wears a bit of jewelry.

All the children stand and eat in silence as their elders talk. Father says he must repair his ax tonight. The ax blade flew off the handle this morning as he chopped wood.

"Flew off the handle"? Your mother accused you of flying off the handle the last time you got angry and lost your temper. This must be where that saying came from!

W hen the meal is over, Father sits back in his chair to review the daily schedules. All the children must help clean the sheep's wool before it can be spun and dyed. The girls will have to make candles and churn butter.

Father and the boys head outside to clear a field. Stones and stumps must be removed before the next corn crop can be planted.

No one questions the jobs they're told to do. Everyone has to work hard and cooperate in order to survive.

All the children have work to do. But today is Tuesday. Do you wonder why they are not in school?

Just then you hear Mother asking Charity to get the horn book. You watch as the little girl dutifully picks up a wooden paddle that has a page with the alphabet attached to it. A thin piece of animal horn covers the whole paddle. It helps keep the page neat and clear. You can see right through the horn. It's like a clear, plastic cover. As the mother knits, Charity sits next to her and practices saying the alphabet.

The women settle in for a little conversation as they work. Mother tells Grandmother that the town has hired a new teacher.

Grandmother shakes her head. The boys will have to wait until the middle of winter before they can attend school. There is too much work they must do around the farm. Besides, the real learning happens right here at home. Girls must learn how to keep house. Boys must learn how to farm. Otherwise, how will they get by when they are adults?

You watch as the mother gives a polite nod. Then she gets up to light a candle. Like you, she has noticed how dark the house has become.

Just then you hear a clap of thunder. Father and the boys scramble through the door. They are all wet and cold from a sudden downpour. Ezra is very excited. The news is out. There will be a corn husking at the Jones farm this Saturday. All the neighbors will help husk the entire corn crop. There's sure to be singing, tasty food, and games for everyone.

While the family listens to Ezra's news, you listen to the rain. The downpour has become a steady drizzle. It's time for you to head forward in time, back to your own family.

You quietly slip out the door. A sweet smell of rain mixes with curls of chimney smoke in the autumn breeze. Change is in the wind too. The coming years will see the arrival of revolution, modern inventions, and new ideas.

Colonial life will soon disappear. Little will remain of Ezra and his family's daily schedules. But not all will be lost. Those old shoes in the museum will still be there to remind us of Ezra, Charity, and their lives in colonial New England.